VIA Folios 143

The Good for the Good

The Good for the Good

Maria Famà

BORDIGHERA PRESS

© 2019 by Maria Famà

Cover art by Rosario Famà
Sicilian Street Scene from a Window

Library of Congress Control Number: 2019943148

Printed in the United States.

Published by
BORDIGHERA PRESS
John D. Calandra Italian American Institute
25 West 43rd Street, 17th Floor
New York, NY 10036

VIA Folios 143
ISBN 978-1-59954-148-8

CONTENTS

This book is dedicated to the memory of poet, translator, scholar, and friend
GIL FAGIANI
who encouraged me to undertake this project.

From my earliest years, I heard sayings, proverbs, and phrases pronounced by my parents, grandparents, family members, and friends, either in Sicilian or Standard Italian. These pithy words are filled with wisdom. They display a keen understanding of human nature and teach a way to live in the world.

When the late poet, scholar, translator, and friend, Gil Fagiani, heard me read my poem, *Tip the Hat You Got*, from my book, *Mystics in the Family*, published by Bordighera Press in 2013, he encouraged me to write a whole book of poems based on these sayings.

I took Gil's good advice and have attempted to use some sayings and phrases as jumping off points to tell some stories through my poetry.

REMEDIES

C'è un rimedio per tutto
There's a remedy for everything
My father used to say
~drink hot water and lemon juice for a bellyache
~have a glass of hot wine with orange slices for a cold
~eat lupini to keep blood sugar low
~chew raw garlic to keep blood pressure down
~massage your skin with olive oil to cure a rash
~stick strips of cucumber peels on your forehead to cool off from
    summer's heat
C'è un rimedio per tutto
There's a remedy for everything
with time   with effort
the right remedy can be found
~chew roasted chickpeas to stave off hunger
~pour breast milk into painful ears
~use a gauze wrapped, olive oil soaked, garlic clove to ease yeast
infections
~dab vinegar on bug bites
~chew fava beans for energy and regularity, too
~remove malocchio headaches with water, salt, olive oil, and special
    prayers
C'è un rimedio per tutto
There's a remedy for everything
with prayers   with practicality
the right remedy can be found
there is only one exception
my father used to say
there is no remedy for death.

TIP THE HAT YOU GOT

Saluta cu cappeddu chi hai
my grandfather, Pietro Guaetta, used to say

I called him Grandpop
my loving, patient, Sicilian grandfather
always answered all my questions

Grandpop, I asked,
What does saluta cu cappeddu chi hai mean?

He said
Saluta cu cappeddu chi hai
Tip the hat you got

Grandpop, what does that mean?

He said
if you got on a little cap
    you tip your little cap
if you got on a great, big, Texas ten gallon hat
    you tip your great, big, Texas ten gallon hat
if you got on a top hat, straw hat, or derby
    you tip your top hat, straw hat, or derby

Grandpop, what does that mean?

He said
Saluta cu cappeddu chi hai

Tip the hat you got
If you are poor
If you are rich
It does not matter
Respect yourself
Respect others

Do your best with what you got

Saluta cu cappeddu chi hai
Tip the hat you got.

THE GOOD FOR THE GOOD

Three years after the end of World War II
two years after she'd come to America
my grandmother, Maria Concetta,
found herself riding in a limousine
at her son's wedding
she rode with her husband and the bride's parents
all of them from San Pier Niceto, Sicilia
Maria Concetta, the latest to arrive in America

The bride's mother, my grandmother, Domenica,
complimented Maria Concetta on her stylish new hat
Maria Concetta replied
"I Boni Pi I Boni"
The Good For The Good
shocking Domenica
who expected a thank you from her paesana, now her comare,
not such a statement of pride, of arrogance

Yet, Maria Concetta had spoken the truth
she had lived
I Boni Pi I Boni
The Good For The Good

When the Fascists demanded every woman's wedding ring
for the war in Ethiopia
Maria Concetta buried in a secret place
her golden ring, memento of her husband,
far away in America,
she dropped gold earrings

into the helmet in the piazza
telling Fascist officials
she'd lost the ring
washing clothes in the stream
the officials threatened
"If you are lying, remember,
your children are in our school
we can hurt them"
she stood firm   steely eyed
I Boni Pi I Boni
The Good For The Good
her good wedding ring would not
be melted down for evil

Maria Concetta dyed her sons' shirts black
so they could march in the piazza
reciting the Fascist pledge
to shed blood for the fatherland
but she begged her husband
to get them out of Italy
he scraped enough money for two one-way fares
just before the second world war came, shutting down
travel and communication between enemy lands
Maria Concetta and her daughter remained in Sicily
all through the war
each night as the Allied bombs fell
Maria Concetta told her daughter
"Say an Act of Contrition. Tonight we might die"
her husband in New Jersey
her sons now American soldiers fighting somewhere

she held onto the idea that good would triumph
she and her daughter would survive through her efforts
with the Madonna's help the family would reunite
I Boni Pi I Boni
The Good for The Good

After one severe bombing, word spread
an orange grove had been hit, the owners gone,
Maria Concetta trekked to the grove
Everywhere on the charred ground
ripe oranges
I Boni Pi I Boni
The Good For The Good
she picked as many oranges
that fit into the large sack
she carried home on her head
for a while, she and her daughter
ate one good orange a day

Maria Concetta farmed a little plot
though the Germans took most of her crops
she raised a few chickens until Fascists officials
declared all chickens must be killed due to an avian flu
Maria Concetta hid one illegal hen
under the kitchen sink
her daughter feared her mother
would be arrested
Maria Concetta just said
I Boni Pi I Boni
The Good For The Good

they had one egg a day
from a good chicken who lived and survived
with good people

At war's end
mail to and from the USA was restored
Maria Concetta was the first
to receive a package from her husband
news filled the town
neighbors marched with her to the Post Office
escorting her back to her home
her husband had sent
flour, coffee, Hershey's chocolate kisses
she shared what she could
with neighbors crammed into her house
I Boni Pi I Boni
The Good For The Good

In 1946, Maria Concetta and her teenaged daughter
journeyed to America
arriving at her husband's
big, comfortable, New Jersey home
filled with modern appliances
I Boni Pi I Boni
The Good For The Good
from then on,
Maria Concetta never ate a leftover
she bought the best shoes, dresses, coats, hats
never even waiting for a sale
I Boni Pi I Boni
The Good For The Good

Riding in that limousine
at her son's wedding
Maria Concetta was triumphant
her remark to a compliment
became a family legend
I Boni Pi I Boni
The Good For The Good
Maria Concetta understood
that in her life
good had indeed trumped evil
I Boni Pi I Boni
The Good For The Good.

'U SULI È N'AUTRU CUMPAGNU

The rains came in May when
I planted basil, rosemary, tomatoes,
longing for the sun
which Nonno Pietro told his children
was another companion
peering up at the dark clouds, I thought of
my Grandpop Pete telling me
how he cried for Sicilian sunshine
when he worked Pennsylvania coalmines

'U Suli è n'autru cumpagnu
The Sun is another companion
　　　　who heats Sicily's fountains
　　　　kisses Southwest canyons
　　　　warms Hawaiian palms
'O Sole Mio di Napoli
'U Suli di Sicilia
Our good star Sol
our other companion blazes on Zia Antonia's balcony
dries my wash on a South Philly clothesline

We know nurturing rains must fall on us all
basil, bees, daisies, cherries, beans, bears, and frogs
all of us flora　　all of us fauna
Our star is always with us
though by day we long to see his full face
'U Suli è n'autru cumpagnu
The Sun is another companion.

CU GESÙ MI CURCU

As my grandmother lay dying
my mother held her mother's hand
together they recited
Cu Gesù mi curcu
Cu Gesù mi staiu
Stannu cu Gesù paura no nnaiu
A child's prayer of safety of comfort
Cu Gesù mi curcu
with Jesus I fall asleep
passed down through generations
to say before bed
Cu Gesù mi staiu
with Jesus I stay
Stannu cu Gesù paura no nnaiu
staying with Jesus I'm not afraid
from nighttime to daylight
from daylight to eternal light
from one life to another
Cu Gesù mi curcu
Cu Gesù mi staiu
Stannu cu Gesù paura no nnaiu
a child's prayer of safety of comfort
I've chanted in the dark
every night for six decades
Cu Gesù mi curcu
Cu Gesù mi staiu
Stannu cu Gesù paura no nnaiu.

FORTI IMPEDIMENTI

"Forti impedimenti"
when I was a young girl I chafed against those words
whenever my mother said them
When I told her I wanted to go to university
"Forti impedimenti"
When I told her I hoped to get a new job
"Forti impedimenti"
When I told her I planned on traveling abroad
"Forti impedimenti"

I fought against those words   I'd say
Ma, why are you saying forti impedimenti to every wish, desire, or
plan I have?
My mother explained that she said "Forti impedimenti"
so that strong barriers, obstacles, impediments be put in my path
if my wish, desire, or plan would bring me harm
I realized then that my mother's "Forti impedimenti"
was her way of safeguarding me, was her fervent prayer
that only what was best for me would happen

Now, in my elder years, even I can say, "Forti impedimenti"
to every wish, desire, or plan.

MEGGHIU SULA CA MALA ACCUPAGNATA

My family always celebrated Valentine's Day
my mother and grandmother decorated their homes
with cupids and hearts, sent out cards,
baked heart-shaped sugar cakes

My father always bought my mother jewelry with a card
My grandfather always bought my grandmother
 a frilly box of chocolates with a card
each child got pretty cards
ate Valentine cake and candy

A few days before Valentine's Day
filled with love's joyful spirit
I sat at the kitchen table writing
dime-store valentines for
my parents, grandparents, brothers, cousins, aunts, uncles,
and classmates

I mailed my classmates' cards in
the big red classroom mailbox
On Valentine's Day, we sat with our hands folded
as the teacher walked up and down the aisles
placing cards on our desks

When I was in the fourth grade
I watched as cards piled up on my classmates' desks
I got only one card that year
Signed "Guess Who?" in perfect penmanship
I knew it was from the teacher

At home, amidst cupids and cake
I cried
my parents and grandparents said
"Megghiu sula ca mala accumpagnata"
Better alone than badly accompanied
You do not need those bad companions at your school
Megghiu sula ca mala accumpagnata
When you grow up
do not ever settle for unfaithful friends
do not ever pick an abusive spouse
do not ever be afraid to be alone
Better alone than badly accompanied

Over the years.
I have treasured all the Valentines I have gotten
the joy of love prevails
Megghiu sula ca mala accumpagnata
True Valentines do come.

THE BEST WORD IS THE ONE YOU DON'T SAY

'A megghia parola è chidda ca nun si dici
The best word is the one you don't say
this oft-repeated dictum echoes in my head and I wonder
how can I be a poet and learn from this advice?

'A megghia parola è chidda ca nun si dici
served us well in the land of omertà
    hold one's tongue
    be secretive
    be taciturn
    the utterance of the word
    the pronouncement of the word
    might harm
    might damn
    might be fatal

Mindful that words have consequences
I will not say the best word out loud
I will preserve it by writing it down
Make a poem to take away the sting of
'A megghia parola è chidda ca nun si dici

The best word is not the one you don't say
It is the one you write.

CUORE DI LEONE
In memory of Francesco Famà

Nonno Frank used to say
"When you drive, you need a cuore di leone"
I think you need a lion's heart always
even when you just walk

Nonno Frank left his Sicilian town as a teen
for Pennsylvania coalmines
returned home to fight for Italy
in the First World War
survived the trenches, married, fathered children
crossed the ocean again and again
torn between making money in America and
his homesickness for Sicily
he went back and forth
Sicilia to USA   USA to Sicilia   Sicilia to USA
until the Great Depression
trapped him in America
broke, living in an attic, doing odd jobs
far from his wife and children
he needed a cuore di leone to find the courage
to live for years alone until he could see his family again
after the Second World War

I tap along with my cane on city streets as
I dodge cars, bikes, coaches, buses, beggars, and texters
I never fought on the frontlines of battle
my trips abroad were joyous

my cares and worries are ordinary
my family is near
yet, I hope I have a cuore di leone, too

Nonno Frank found a job with Mack Trucks
during WWII but he never owned a car
he walked everywhere

I write and teach
used to have a car but sold it
when I could no longer afford the fees
I walk everywhere

Now, each evening, I hope my lion's heart beats true
when I walk the gauntlet of beggars
who scream their needs in my face
curse and insult me as I make my way home

Nonno Frank faced life's struggles firm and stoic
with his lion's heart
I hope to do the same
Today, his granddaughter amends his words:
"When you live, you need a cuore di leone."

QUANNU QUANNU

Quannu quannu nesce Fra Santu
Whenever Fra Santu went out

When we heard these words
from parents, grandparents, aunts, uncles, cousins
we knew
that we good people had gone out from our homes
for a special occasion
only to have fate deal us a nasty blow
late trains
thunderstorms
headaches
sick children
flat tires

Quannu Quannu
that is all they had to say
we knew what it meant
Fra Santu was a Sicilian monk
who met disasters whenever he left the monastery
quannu quannu nesce Fra Santu
whenever Fra Santu went out
he'd fall and break his leg
a tree limb would knock him unconscious
an earthquake struck
the bridge washed out
his donkey fainted
Quannu quannu nesce Fra Santu
my parents, grandparents, aunts, uncles, cousins,

my brothers and me

when we ventured outside our homes

for a special occasion

we became like Fra Santu

Quannu quannu

half way to an out of town wedding

our car, packed with seven fancy dressed people,

broke down

Quannu quannu

at the graduation party

at the birthday party

at the anniversary party

dizziness   a migraine   nausea

strep throat   bronchitis   influenza   would   strike

Quannu quannu

on a paid vacation to Williamsburg

my father's crippling gout flared up

Quannu quannu

viewing the mosaics at Piazza Armerina

my mother suffered violent cramps

Quannu quannu

during a trip to Niagara Falls

my brother got trench mouth

Quannu quannu

on my way to my book reception and reading

the bus stalled for three hours

outside the Lincoln Tunnel

Quannu quannu nesce Fra Santu

snowstorms   car crashes   hurricanes

Quannu quannu any of us goes out from our homes

fate lies in wait.

VEDENDO, FACENDO

My parents never made reservations
for family vacations
vedendo, facendo
seeing, doing
was their motto
they'd figure out what to do
when they saw where they were
vedendo, facendo
with a car full of kids
late at night
Daddy drove for hours past
No Vacancy motel signs
until he finally saw a place to stay
vedendo, facendo
seeing, doing
you never know what you'll do
until you see the situation

If we asked our father
Daddy, can you take us to the carnival?
He'd answer vedendo, facendo
Daddy, can you get us a toy?
Vedendo, facendo
Daddy, can you buy us french fries?
Vedendo, facendo

My brothers thought that
when Daddy said vedendo, facendo

it meant NO
but I was hopeful

vedendo, facendo
seeing, doing
we might go to the carnival
get toys, eat french fries

vedendo, facendo
seeing, doing
anything could happen.

BIRD IN THE FIG TREE

The grey feathered bird sits in a September fig tree
next to a window in a South Philadelphia backyard
he whistles, chirps, and warbles, singing his own songs
in time to Neapolitan music I play on compact disc

Santa Lucia Lontana

           How far are we really, little friend,
           from the Mediterranean shore?

I' Te Vurria Vasà

           Sure voiced creature, how many kisses
           can you earn with a song?

Tu Ca Nun Chiagne

           Do you cry for those not with you?
           Do others long for you?

Grey feathered one, you feast on the season's last figs
between songs as I change the disc

Piscatore 'E Pusilleco

           Your wings lift you to where
           there is sun and sea

The fig tree will be covered soon
the snow will come
you will sing with full heart
in another part of the world.

SALE

Sah lay   Sah lay   Sah lay
When my father first came to America
he wondered why Americans needed so much salt
sah lay   sah lay   sah lay
there were signs everywhere for
sah lay   sah lay   sah lay

One day while they walked
through downtown New Brunswick, New Jersey
my father asked his father who'd been in the States awhile
"Why does every store in America sell salt?
Even clothing stores sell salt!"
My grandfather puzzled over this
"They don't sell salt in clothing stores"
My father pointed to all the signs
in all the store windows   "Look!
It says sah lay in the shoe store
        sah   lay in the dress shop
        sah   lay in the hardware store"

sah lay   sah lay   sah lay
Nonno said
"You are reading the Italian word sah lay
but this is the English word say   el
It looks the same: S A L E
you say it different

it means discount

say el   say el   say el

No sah lay in these stores

Only a say el   say el   say el."

NUN PROMETTIRI A SANTI E PICCIRIDDI

Don't Make Promises to Saints and Children
When I was a little girl
every year in late summer
a man with a mahogany arm visited
collecting money for the poor
in honor of San Nicola da Tolentino

He sat at our kitchen table
sipping espresso, munching biscotti,
writing into his donation book,
all with his left hand
his richly dark right arm
with the curved hand and
delicate, carved fingernails
sat motionless on the table top

My parents always gave money
we always attended the party
the man with the mahogany arm hosted in September
in honor of Saint Nicholas of Tolentino
in a hall jammed with children and adults
piles of panini, big platters of pasta.,
trays of cookies, tubs of soda and beer on ice,
a bar for whiskey and anisette,
music, dancing, and laughter
the man with the mahogany arm stood
in the center of it all
smiling, joking, singing

his still wooden arm
hanging at his side

When my father told us the story of
the man with the mahogany arm
he began, "Nun promettiri a santi e picciriddi"
Don't make promises to saints and children
When the man with the mahogany arm
was a young man in Italy
he got very sick
he prayed to San Nicola da Tolentino
promising if he got well
he would collect money for the poor and
hold a big feast in the Saint's honor
the man got better   time passed
he forgot his promise to San Nicola
when his right arm began to swell
it had to be cut off
a mahogany arm replaced it
he then remembered his promise
which he fulfilled every year
even when he came to America
he went house to house collecting money for the poor
and honoring the Saint with a big party

"Nun promettiri a santi e picciriddi"
Don't make promises to saints and children
Saints, I knew, were powerful but I asked
How could a child force someone
to keep a promise?

My father explained, "Nun promettiri a santi e picciriddi" because
Children will give you no peace they will keep asking
they will say, "You promised!" over and over
you will wish you never promised

Don't make promises to saints and children
Saints and children expect a promise to be kept
children will annoy in the short term
saints will act in the long term

It is best to heed the advice
"Nun promettiri a santi e picciriddi."

EVERYBODY CRIES WITH THEIR OWN EYES

When I was a child,
I watched my great uncle, Crispino Giacobello,
say his morning prayers
by the light of the window
in Grandmom's big barrel chair
we called our uncle, ZiZi,
a term of great affection,
my grandparents called him, Cugnatu, brother-in-law,
his beloved first wife, Grazia, Grandpop's sister,
died of Spanish flu decades before

ZiZi prayed out loud in Sicilian
clutching his prayer book
big tears rolling down his cheeks
I asked my grandmother why he was crying
she told me
everybody cries with their own eyes
out of sorrow   out of fear   out of pain
some cry because they have too little
others cry because they have too much
some cry out of hunger   frustration   loneliness
everybody cries with their own eyes

When ZiZi prayed
he held onto Grazia's wedding ring
in his pocket all his life
my grandparents took ZiZi in
when he had nowhere to go

he saved their house during the Great Depression
with his Conservation Corps salary
his second marriage ended in divorce
his bombardier son died in World War II

When I was little
ZiZi was in his sixties
Jolly with merry eyes
he laughed and laughed at anything
we children did or said
ZiZi babysat us
sometimes walked us to school
holding our hands so tight
making sure we did not get hit
by a "machine"
translating the Italian for car, "macchina,"
into English for us
ZiZi sometimes laughed when we cried
over a playmate's snub or parent's reprimand
we got mad at him   he laughed harder
his eyes twinkled
ZiZi cried with his own eyes
everyday at his morning prayers
Grandmom said
In life we all get chances to laugh
and chances to cry
yet we all must cry with our own eyes.

MAY YOUR EYES GO UP YOUR ASS

If you suspect someone of giving you the malocchio
Here is a quick way to prevent that evil eye from harming you:
Place your left hand in your pocket
Point your pinky and pointer fingers straight down
other fingers curled into the palm
say silently in your head to that person of the evil eye
"May your eyes go up your ass."
Boomerang to you
mean young girl who shouts, "Fat Bitch!"
to passersby
May your eyes go up your ass.
Boomerang to you
tall man with an expensive haircut
who grabs persons to yell in their faces about hell
May your eyes go up your ass.
Boomerang to you
tough blonde lady in rolled-up tee shirt
demanding money with a snarl
May your eyes go up your ass.
Boomerang to you all
the meanness   the disrespect   the envy
that propel your malocchio
May your eyes go up your ass
Be sure to enjoy the view.

CHICKPEAS

This is how we pass down our history
Hold up a handful of chickpeas
Say "cìceri" in Sicilian tongue

This is how we pass down our history
through the ages
whether we could read or write or not
in countryside   mountainside   seaside

This is how we pass down our history
my father holds up a handful of roasted chickpeas
makes us repeat the word after him
"cìceri"   "cìceri"   "cìceri"
we are children anxious to leave the table
play   laugh   shout   in English
in Philadelphia   USA
where our family set down roots
fragile and tough as chickpea plants

we were Mediterranean for millennia
            American for two decades

This is how we pass down our history
my father holds up a handful of roasted chickpeas
this night they are snacks with wine
my grandfather tells us we should always have
a handful of chickpeas in our pocket as he does
in case we get hungry

in case we are served food we cannot eat
the chickpeas will sustain us
"cìceri"   "cìceri"   "cìceri"

My father holds up a handful of chickpeas
this humble   exalted   Mediterranean food
in a Philadelphia kitchen
we must learn to say
"cìceri"   "cìceri"   "cìceri"

This is how we pass down our history
over the centuries   across oceans
countryside   mountainside   seaside
My father tells us the history of the proud and oppressed
In 1282 the Sicilians rose up
against the arrogant haughty French
who taxed and insulted the Sicilian people
took liberties with Sicilian women
lounged in Sicilian homes

Sicilians were patient   waiting for their chance
to overthrow the French
the chance came on Easter Monday in Palermo
in front of the Church of the Holy Spirit
the armed French soldiers stood guard
over the Palermitans thronging the piazza
as they headed to the Church's Vespers service
the French soldier, Drouette, filled with Sicilian wine,
stopped a beautiful young woman
walking to church with her husband

Drouette grabbed her as if to search for weapons
fondled her breasts
her husband shouted   "Death to the French!"
the crowd surged   the fighting began
Drouette fell   stabbed in the heart

Messengers carried the signal throughout the island
the time had come   "Death to the French!"
Sicilians rose up
With knives, rocks, sticks, stones, canes, swords
west to east   east to west
north to south   south to north
"Death to the French!"
Thousands of French hunted down and killed
as the signal traveled the island's
countryside   mountainside   seaside
My father tells us some French tried to escape
dressed in peasant clothes
they hid in countryside   mountainside   seaside
they were caught and killed my father says
my grandfather holds up a handful of chickpeas
says "cìceri"   "cìceri"   "cìceri"
my father says the French could not pronounce the word correctly
"cìceri"   "cìceri"   "cìceri"
humble   exalted   powerful   chickpeas
"cìceri"   "cìceri"   "cìceri"

If you were Sicilian you said "cìceri"
if you were Sicilian
Go in Peace   The Madonna Bless You

in your countryside   mountainside   seaside   home
you lived on to bless
the exalted   humble   powerful
"cìceri"   "cìceri"   "cìceri"

This is how we pass down our history
my father and grandfather holding chickpeas in their palms
telling us how Sicilians chopped up French dead
shipped them back to France pickled in barrels

our skin goosebumps as we listen
our eyes widen with horror and wonder

think how it would be if Sicilians held up chickpeas
they would kill you if you did not say it right
"cìceri"   "cìceri"   "cìceri"
you feel sorry for those French
sent to a faraway land where they were hated
where they could not pronounce
"cìceri"   "cìceri"   "cìceri"

you feel relief as you say
"cìceri"   "cìceri"   "cìceri"
you would live and be sustained by
humble   exalted   powerful   chickpeas

you are proud
as you take a handful of roasted chickpeas
eat them slowly
your father and grandfather smile

when you say "cìceri"   "cìceri"   "cìceri"
because even though you live in Philadelphia USA
your family was saved nearly eight hundred years ago
in countryside   mountainside   seaside
when they said "cìceri"   "cìceri"   "cìceri"

Therefore, this is how we must pass down our history
hold up a handful of chickpea
say "cìceri" in Sicilian tongue.

PIDUCCHIUSU, PIDUCCHIUSU

When someone insists on a detail
to the point of exasperating others
when someone won't back down
even when at risk
it is said that person is "piduchhiusu, piducchiusu"
Cousin Minnie Fareri once told me why:
A long time ago in Sicily
an old lady insulted a magistrate's dignity
by telling him to his face that
he was lice-infested
"piducchiusu, piducchiusu" she said
The magistrate threatened her
she would not back down
insisting he was "piducchiusu, piducchiusu"
lice-infested, lice-infested
even when the magistrate ordered her
lowered into a well and
she could no longer see her torturers
she threw her arms above her head
making the sign for lice
thumb and pointer fingers touching and pulling away

We don't know the old woman's name
Was she foolish or brave? Or both?
The townspeople still keep her memory alive
with her last words
"piducchiusu, piducchiusu."

CU TANTU SI CALA 'U CULU SI PARA

Our proud Zia Angelina, Aunt Angie on Moore Street,
lover of fine cuisine   cleanliness   grand opera
carried herself like a duchess
always well dressed   imperious   she often said
"Cu tantu si cala 'u culu si para"
if you bend too low your ass will show
she knew that when you bow low
trying to please
kowtowing to others to curry favor
your rear end juts into the air
a stiff kick's target

Aunt Angie advised us to take credit for accomplishment
toot our own horns   brag a little   bluff a little
stand tall at work or at home
scrub brush, dishrag, computer, pen, spoon, shovel,
all worthy tools
no task too menial it does not have value

Aunt Angie taught that abusers are rampant
mistaking humility for weakness
be generous   be flexible   be proud
let no one take advantage

acknowledge   smile   laugh
one can be regal even with a toilet brush as scepter
Remember
Cu tantu si cala 'u culu si para
If you bend too low, your ass will show.

EVERY CHRISTMAS

Ogni Natale
We play Nonno Pietro's old bagpipe records,
the ones he hid under his coat,
until he played them for Nonna so she wouldn't be angry
that he'd spent one whole day's wage
for La Novena di Natale con ciaramella
and another's
for Pastorale con ciaramella
and still another's
for Tu Scendi Dalle Stelle con ciaramella

Ogni Natale
I place the bagpipe player figurine
outside the presepio's stable door
for Gesù Bambino's sweet serenade,
I bought this rosy cheeked player
at the Piazza Navona fair that swirled and pulsed
with bagpipe music on cassette.

Ogni Natale
I recall the December day I followed
wind-blown bagpipers down Rome's fashion lit street
in tears of longing and tears of joy
awed by the skill and moved by the songs.
Ogni Natale
I remember the Christmas Eve I stood
on stark Sicilian mountains
listening with full heart to the yearning ancient sound

of three bagpipes in procession
clear as the nighttime air
brilliant as the Mediterranean stars
profound as the blue black sky.

Ogni Natale
I can know again and understand exactly why
Nonno Pietro paid his wages of toil and
          his wages of pain
to hear la ciaramella's plaintive voice.

DOPO I CONFETTI, I DIFETTI

Boarding the midnight train at Arezzo
Pina and I popped into a compartment
plopped down into seats facing each other
free from school   ready for summer fun in Venezia

By the window
two elderly women sat across from each other
playing cards, munching on bread, cheese, wine, and olives
they offered us some
we said thanks but we were tired not hungry
we slumped down
our jeaned legs stretched across the aisle touching
Pina fell asleep
I closed my eyes   eavesdropped
"Quant'è bella giovinezza!" exclaimed one woman,
quoting none other than Lorenzo de'Medici, il Magnifico,
the other agreed, it was beautiful to be young
look how fast we fell asleep
while sleep eluded them

They had been on the train for hours
traveling from Southern Italy for a wedding
they drew cards   talked of the bride
they met the groom only once   he seemed nice
suddenly both women pronounced in unison
"Dopo i confetti, i difetti"
after the confetti, those sugared almonds
handed out at weddings,

after the dinner, dancing, toasts
the spouses would see each other's defects
get on each other's nerves
learn to live with faults or not

Dopo i confetti, i defetti
After the confetti, the defects
Pina was sound asleep across from me
her right leg relaxed against my left
I kept my eyes closed
we are all flawed
it's a wonder anybody gets along
with anybody else
yet we have to try
        have to love
        have to be patient
        with one another
        because
        dopo i confetti, i difetti.

AMMUCCIA, AMMUCCIA CA TUTTU PARI

Hide, hide, and everything shows

After the Blessed Mother was locked in the church
to spite the priest
Nino Guardia wrote to my mother
that the sanpieroti were
ciangiolini, muccialori, e traditori
our ancestral town was full of
crybabies, sneaks, and traitors

I thought aren't we all?

We hide our mistakes
     our money
    our debt
     our bad habits
    our ages
   our shortcomings
we try to hide
eventually we are found out
ammuccia, ammuccia ca tuttu pari
hide, hide, and everything shows

Angry that the priest changed
Our Lady of Mount Carmel's age-old procession route
some townspeople of San Pier Niceto, Sicilia
met in secret, ranted, raved,
acted in the middle of the night

barricaded the church from the inside and outside
imprisoning the Madonna's statue

The next morning
another group of townspeople.
outraged that some would dare to secretly bar
Our Lady of Mount Carmel from her procession
on her July 16 Feast Day,
borrowed another Blessed Mother statue
from a nearby town
the procession went on as planned
the secret group was found out
barricades removed
the Madonna liberated

Anonymous letters and calls from both groups
flooded the office of the Diocese of Messina
the priest was transferred

Ammuccia, ammuccia ca tuttu pari
Hide, hide, and everything shows.

COMARI

My comari, my co-marys, my co-marias
Comari, Comari, Comari, Comari
we are rich   we are strong
  in comari tradition
comari, comari, comari, comari
My comari, my co-marys, my co-marias,
I tell you now
a story of my Aunt
the story of Zia Angelina
  proud and regal   with burning black eyes
she had a comare
a dear comare
a beautiful comare   a loving comare
Comare Comare Comare Comare Maria
they lived   they lived two
they lived two doors away
  from each other
these comari comari comari comari
  Angelina e Maria
  Maria e Angelina
They passed   they passed
  they passed
they have since passed
  but when
they were alive
they passed flowered china dishes
  filled with delicacies
  to each other

they passed dishes of
  tortellini in brood
  merluzzo in bianco
  insalata d'arugula
these comari comari comari comari
Comare Angelina   Comare Maria
late afternoons they sipped
  they sipped and dipped
  they sipped espresso
  they dipped biscotti
in late afternoons they sipped and dipped
before   before   before
  the husbands
before   before   before
  the suppers
they sipped and dipped
before the suppers and husbands
filled their homes
these comari comari comari comari
They remembered these comari
  each name day
  each birthday
always a greeting card these comari
comari comari comari comari
inside and outside
dishes   coffee   greeting cards
through South Philadelphia streets
far from their Sicilian town
  they made do
  they had to

they made do
with dishes   coffee   greeting cards

Once   once   once
Comare Comare Comare Maria's birthday
her birthday was coming
Comare Comare Comare Angelina
made spumetti
she made spumetti from eggwhites and nuts
eggwhites   and   nuts   and   sugar
sweets for her Comare Comare Comare Maria
then Angelina went
Comare Angelina went   she went
Comare Angelina went to the Avenue to buy a card
a beautiful card   a beautiful birthday card
for her Comare Comare Comare Maria
Angelina read cards that said Happy Birthday
No good   no good   no good
  too plain   too plain
for the beautiful beautiful Comare Comare Comare Maria
Angelina read cards that said Happy Birthday Friend
No good   no good   no good
  no words to describe
the dear, the dearer, the dearest
Comare Comare Comare Maria
Angelina read cards that said Happy Birthday Sister
No good   no good   no good
  too boring   too boring
  not love enough
for the lovely and loving and loved

Comare Comare Comare Maria
Angelina read cards that said Happy Birthday Husband
and there   and there   and there
  was the perfect card
there was the perfect card
for the beautiful, the dear, the loving
Comare Comare Comare Maria

Angelina bought that card
She bought the To My Dear Husband card
she bought it   and loved it
and took it home
where she took a pen   a black pen
she took a black pen
and crossed out Husband
she crossed that word right out
she crossed out Husband   and wrote Comare
  in her Italian script
TO MY DEAR COMARE
the words all fit
the words   inside   and outside
the words all fit
the card   her heart
the words all fit
they fit   she knew they fit
inside and outside
she knew they fit her
Comare Comare Comare Maria
Angelina's Comare Maria.

IETTA SANGU!

My mother hated to hear the curse
Ietta Sangu! Spill your blood!
Comare Felicia, the next-door neighbor,
yelled "Ietta sangu! Ietta sangu!"
everyday at her son, Petie,

A few years younger than Petie,
my mother thought him handsome and charming
yet everyday Felicia's voice
could be heard screaming at Petie
"Ietta sangu! Ietta sangu!"
Petie made his mother so upset
with his childish pranks
raucous games
smart remarks
she'd yell, "Ietta sangu! Ietta sangu" at her son

World War II came
Petie was drafted
killed in action
my mother remembered
Comare Felicia's shrieks
when they got the news
Felicia wept bitter tears
she cried she had killed her son
with her curse "Ietta sangu! Ietta sangu!"
which she screamed at Petie everyday

When Petie's coffin was brought home
my teenaged mother heard in the middle of the night
the sounds of hammers, chisels, crowbars
coming from next door
Comare Felicia and her husband
opened Petie's coffin
blood curdling screams
a father's grief
a mother's guilt
everyday she had yelled
"Ietta sangu! Ietta sangu!

Felicia cursed Petie
to spill his blood and he had.

OGGI IN FIGURA, DOMANI IN SEPOLTURA

Crowds fill the streets
Roads are jammed with traffic
Internet and phones buzz with chatter
Yet like leaves in autumn, we fall
young, old, friend, stranger, family
we leave the burdens of the world
each day obituaries are written
each day funeral parlors are full
each day battlefields are littered with the fallen
each day some drown to get to freedom
others die in their bombed-out home
others lose against hurricane, monsoon, earthquake, tornado,
we leave
from a bed, a car, from mountains, from the city and from the sea

Oggi in figura, domani in sepoltura
Today alive, tomorrow placed in the tomb
Today present and accounted for
Tomorrow
    heart attack
    stroke
    illness
    accident
    one fast day
    many dwindling days

We all must face the end
That is our path
That is our great mystery

Oggi in figura, domani in sepoltura.

MO CHI? MO COM'?

Mario, dear Abruzzese friend,
taught my father the phrase
"Mo chi? Mo com'?
Now who? Now how?
when asked a question you don't like
Mo Chi? Mo Com'?
Now who? Now how?
play disturbed   play confused
Mo chi? Mo com'?
act dumb   act dense
nobody needs to know your business
Mo chi? Mo com'?
when asked to state an opinion you'd rather not
Mo chi? Mo com'?
pretend you cannot hear
the gossiping
the insults
the backbiting
no need to get involved
Mo chi? Mo com'?
Now who? Now how?

PATATI!

Americans say Baloney!
My Sicilian family says Patati!
Potatoes! So humble, so commonplace. Patati!
To politicians' promises
Patati!
To flatterers' compliments
Patati!
To advertisers' claims
Patati!
We are schooled in humility
By Patati
We cannot ever be too proud
With Patati
Someone says he is a CEO
CEO of what? Patati?
You say you won a prize
A prize for what? Patati?
Honorifics?
The Dean of Patati
The Queen of Patati
The Cavaliere of Patati
The Contessa of Patati
The Doctor of Patati
The Bishop of Patati
Potatoes! So humble, so commonplace. Patati!
The world is full of Patati.

*Patati is Sicilian for potatoes, which is Patate in Standard Italian.

ACKNOWLEDGMENTS

Grateful acknowledgement is made to the editors of the following publications in which some of these poems first appeared: *21 Poems, Avanti Popolo!, Ovunque Siamo, Paterson Literary Review,* and *Philadelphia Poets.*

Dopo I Confetti, I Difetti won the 12th Annual John and Rose Petracca Family Award, 2019

Cu Tanto Si Cala 'u Culu Si Para won Second Prize in the 2018 Allen Ginsberg Poetry Awards.

Cuore di Leone (2015) and *Cu Gesù Mi Curcu* (2017) were Editor's Choice selections in the Allen Ginsberg Awards.

ABOUT THE AUTHOR

MARIA FAMÀ is the author of seven books of poetry. Her work appears in numerous publications and anthologies. In 2018, she was the Second Prize Winner in the Allen Ginsberg Poetry Awards. Of Sicilian descent, Famà has read her poetry in many cities across the United States and recorded her poems for CD compilations of music and poetry. She appears reading her poetry in the films *Prisoners Among Us*, *Pipes of Peace*, and *La Mia Strada*. Her most recent books are *Other Nations: an animal journal*, published in 2017 by Pearlsong Press and *Mystics in the Family*, published by Bordighera Press in 2013. Maria Famà lives and works in Philadelphia, PA.

VIA FOLIOS

A refereed book series dedicated to the culture of Italians and Italian Americans.

ROSEMARY CAPPELLO. *Wonderful Disaster*. Vol. 142. Poetry. $14

B. AMORE. *Journeys on the Wheel*. Vol. 141. Poetry. $14

ALDO PALAZZESCHI. *The Manifestos of Aldo Palazzeschi*. Vol 140. Literature. $14

ROSS TALARICO. *The Reckoning*. Vol 139. Poetry. $24

MICHELLE REALE. *Season of Subtraction*. Vol 138. Poetry. $8

MARISA FRASCA. *Wild Fennel*. Vol 137. Poetry. $10

RITA ESPOSITO WATSON. *Italian Kisses*. Vol. 136. Memoir. $14

SARA FRUNER. *Bitter Bites from Sugar Hills*. Vol. 135. Poetry. $12

KATHY CURTO. *Not for Nothing*. Vol. 134. Memoir. $16

JENNIFER MARTELLI. *My Tarantella*. Vol. 133. Poetry. $10

MARIA TERRONE. *At Home in the New World*. Vol. 132. Essays. $16

GIL FAGIANI. *Missing Madonnas*. Vol. 131. Poetry. $14

LEWIS TURCO. *The Sonnetarium*. Vol. 130. Poetry. $12

JOE AMATO. *Samuel Taylor's Hollywood Adventure*. Vol. 129. Novel. $20

BEA TUSIANI. *Con Amore*. Vol. 128. Memoir. $16

MARIA GIURA. *What My Father Taught Me*. Vol. 127. Poetry. $12

STANISLAO PUGLIESE. *A Century of Sinatra*. Vol. 126. Popular Culture. $12

TONY ARDIZZONE. *The Arab's Ox*. Vol. 125. Novel. $18

PHYLLIS CAPELLO. *Packs Small Plays Big*. Vol. 124. Literature.

FRED GARDAPHÉ. *Read 'em and Reap*. Vol. 123. Criticism. $22

JOSEPH A. AMATO. *Diagnostics*. Vol 122. Literature. $12.

DENNIS BARONE. *Second Thoughts*. Vol 121. Poetry. $10

OLIVIA K. CERRONE. *The Hunger Saint*. Vol 120. Novella. $12

GARIBLADI M. LAPOLLA. *Miss Rollins in Love*. Vol 119. Novel. $24

JOSEPH TUSIANI. *A Clarion Call*. Vol 118. Poetry. $16

JOSEPH A. AMATO. *My Three Sicilies*. Vol 117. Poetry & Prose. $17

MARGHERITA COSTA. *Voice of a Virtuosa and Coutesan*. Vol 116. Poetry. $24

NICOLE SANTALUCIA. *Because I Did Not Die*. Vol 115. Poetry. $12

MARK CIABATTARI. *Preludes to History*. Vol 114. Poetry. $12

HELEN BAROLINI. *Visits*. Vol 113. Novel. $22

ERNESTO LIVORNI. *The Fathers' America*. Vol 112. Poetry. $14

MARIO B. MIGNONE. *The Story of My People*. Vol 111. Non-fiction. $17

GEORGE GUIDA. *The Sleeping Gulf*. Vol 110. Poetry. $14

JOEY NICOLETTI. *Reverse Graffiti*. Vol 109. Poetry. $14

GIOSE RIMANELLI. *Il mestiere del furbo*. Vol 108. Criticism. $20

LEWIS TURCO. *The Hero Enkidu*. Vol 107. Poetry. $14

AL TACCONELLI. *Perhaps Fly*. Vol 106. Poetry. $14

RACHEL GUIDO DEVRIES. *A Woman Unknown in Her Bones*. Vol 105. Poetry. $11

BERNARD BRUNO. *A Tear and a Tear in My Heart*. Vol 104. Non-fiction. $20

FELIX STEFANILE. *Songs of the Sparrow*. Vol 103. Poetry. $30

FRANK POLIZZI. *A New Life with Bianca*. Vol 102. Poetry. $10

GIL FAGIANI. *Stone Walls*. Vol 101. Poetry. $14

LOUISE DESALVO. *Casting Off*. Vol 100. Fiction. $22

MARY JO BONA. *I Stop Waiting for You*. Vol 99. Poetry. $12

RACHEL GUIDO DEVRIES. *Stati zitt, Josie*. Vol 98. Children's Literature. $8

GRACE CAVALIERI. *The Mandate of Heaven*. Vol 97. Poetry. $14

MARISA FRASCA. *Via incanto*. Vol 96. Poetry. $12

DOUGLAS GLADSTONE. *Carving a Niche for Himself*. Vol 95. History. $12

MARIA TERRONE. *Eye to Eye*. Vol 94. Poetry. $14

CONSTANCE SANCETTA. *Here in Cerchio*. Vol 93. Local History. $15

MARIA MAZZIOTTI GILLAN. *Ancestors' Song*. Vol 92. Poetry. $14

MICHAEL PARENTI. *Waiting for Yesterday: Pages from a Street Kid's Life*. Vol 90. Memoir. $15

ANNIE LANZILLOTTO. *Schistsong*. Vol 89. Poetry. $15

EMANUEL DI PASQUALE. *Love Lines*. Vol 88. Poetry. $10

CAROSONE & LOGIUDICE. *Our Naked Lives*. Vol 87. Essays. $15

JAMES PERICONI. *Strangers in a Strange Land: A Survey of Italian-Language American Books*.Vol 86. Book History. $24

DANIELA GIOSEFFI. *Escaping La Vita Della Cucina*. Vol 85. Essays. $22

MARIA FAMÀ. *Mystics in the Family*. Vol 84. Poetry. $10

ROSSANA DEL ZIO. *From Bread and Tomatoes to Zuppa di Pesce "Ciambotto"*.Vol. 83. $15

LORENZO DELBOCA. *Polentoni*. Vol 82. Italian Studies. $15

SAMUEL GHELLI. *A Reference Grammar*. Vol 81. Italian Language. $36

ROSS TALARICO. *Sled Run*. Vol 80. Fiction. $15

FRED MISURELLA. *Only Sons*. Vol 79. Fiction. $14

FRANK LENTRICCHIA. *The Portable Lentricchia*. Vol 78. Fiction. $16

RICHARD VETERE. *The Other Colors in a Snow Storm*. Vol 77. Poetry. $10

GARIBALDI LAPOLLA. *Fire in the Flesh*. Vol 76 Fiction & Criticism. $25

GEORGE GUIDA. *The Pope Stories*. Vol 75 Prose. $15

ROBERT VISCUSI. *Ellis Island*. Vol 74. Poetry. $28

ELENA GIANINI BELOTTI. *The Bitter Taste of Strangers Bread*. Vol 73. Fiction. $24

PINO APRILE. *Terroni*. Vol 72. Italian Studies. $20

EMANUEL DI PASQUALE. *Harvest*. Vol 71. Poetry. $10

ROBERT ZWEIG. *Return to Naples*. Vol 70. Memoir. $16

AIROS & CAPPELLI. *Guido*. Vol 69. Italian/American Studies. $12

FRED GARDAPHÉ. *Moustache Pete is Dead! Long Live Moustache Pete!*. Vol 67. Literature/Oral History. $12

PAOLO RUFFILLI. *Dark Room/Camera oscura*. Vol 66. Poetry. $11

HELEN BAROLINI. *Crossing the Alps*. Vol 65. Fiction. $14

COSMO FERRARA. *Profiles of Italian Americans*. Vol 64. Italian Americana. $16

GIL FAGIANI. *Chianti in Connecticut*. Vol 63. Poetry. $10

BASSETTI & D'ACQUINO. *Italic Lessons*. Vol 62. Italian/American Studies. $10

CAVALIERI & PASCARELLI, Eds. *The Poet's Cookbook*. Vol 61. Poetry/ Recipes. $12

EMANUEL DI PASQUALE. *Siciliana*. Vol 60. Poetry. $8

NATALIA COSTA, Ed. *Bufalini*. Vol 59. Poetry. $18.

RICHARD VETERE. *Baroque*. Vol 58. Fiction. $18.

LEWIS TURCO. *La Famiglia/The Family*. Vol 57. Memoir. $15

NICK JAMES MILETI. *The Unscrupulous*. Vol 56. Humanities. $20

BASSETTI. ACCOLLA. D'AQUINO. *Italici: An Encounter with Piero Bassetti*. Vol 55. Italian Studies. $8

GIOSE RIMANELLI. *The Three-legged One*. Vol 54. Fiction. $15

CHARLES KLOPP. *Bele Antiche Stòrie*. Vol 53. Criticism. $25

JOSEPH RICAPITO. *Second Wave*. Vol 52. Poetry. $12

GARY MORMINO. *Italians in Florida*. Vol 51. History. $15

GIANFRANCO ANGELUCCI. *Federico F.* Vol 50. Fiction. $15

ANTHONY VALERIO. *The Little Sailor*. Vol 49. Memoir. $9

ROSS TALARICO. *The Reptilian Interludes*. Vol 48. Poetry. $15

RACHEL GUIDO DE VRIES. *Teeny Tiny Tino's Fishing Story*. Vol 47. Children's Literature. $6

EMANUEL DI PASQUALE. *Writing Anew*. Vol 46. Poetry. $15

MARIA FAMÀ. *Looking For Cover*. Vol 45. Poetry. $12

ANTHONY VALERIO. *Toni Cade Bambara's One Sicilian Night*. Vol 44. Poetry. $10

EMANUEL CARNEVALI. *Furnished Rooms*. Vol 43. Poetry. $14

BRENT ADKINS. et al., Ed. *Shifting Borders. Negotiating Places*. Vol 42. Conference. $18

GEORGE GUIDA. *Low Italian*. Vol 41. Poetry. $11

GARDAPHÈ, GIORDANO, TAMBURRI. *Introducing Italian Americana*. Vol 40. Italian/American Studies. $10

DANIELA GIOSEFFI. *Blood Autumn/Autunno di sangue*. Vol 39. Poetry. $15/$25

FRED MISURELLA. *Lies to Live By*. Vol 38. Stories. $15

STEVEN BELLUSCIO. *Constructing a Bibliography*. Vol 37. Italian Americana. $15

ANTHONY JULIAN TAMBURRI, Ed. *Italian Cultural Studies 2002*. Vol 36. Essays. $18

BEA TUSIANI. *con amore*. Vol 35. Memoir. $19

FLAVIA BRIZIO-SKOV, Ed. *Reconstructing Societies in the Aftermath of War*. Vol 34. History. $30

TAMBURRI. et al., Eds. *Italian Cultural Studies 2001*. Vol 33. Essays. $18

ELIZABETH G. MESSINA, Ed. *In Our Own Voices*. Vol 32. Italian/American Studies. $25

STANISLAO G. PUGLIESE. *Desperate Inscriptions*. Vol 31. History. $12

HOSTERT & TAMBURRI, Eds. *Screening Ethnicity*. Vol 30. Italian/American Culture. $25

G. PARATI & B. LAWTON, Eds. *Italian Cultural Studies*. Vol 29. Essays. $18

HELEN BAROLINI. *More Italian Hours*. Vol 28. Fiction. $16

FRANCO NASI, Ed. *Intorno alla Via Emilia*. Vol 27. Culture. $16

ARTHUR L. CLEMENTS. *The Book of Madness & Love*. Vol 26. Poetry. $10

JOHN CASEY, et al. *Imagining Humanity*. Vol 25. Interdisciplinary Studies. $18

ROBERT LIMA. *Sardinia/Sardegna*. Vol 24. Poetry. $10

DANIELA GIOSEFFI. *Going On*. Vol 23. Poetry. $10

ROSS TALARICO. *The Journey Home*. Vol 22. Poetry. $12

EMANUEL DI PASQUALE. *The Silver Lake Love Poems*. Vol 21. Poetry. $7

JOSEPH TUSIANI. *Ethnicity*. Vol 20. Poetry. $12

JENNIFER LAGIER. *Second Class Citizen*. Vol 19. Poetry. $8

FELIX STEFANILE. *The Country of Absence*. Vol 18. Poetry. $9

PHILIP CANNISTRARO. *Blackshirts*. Vol 17. History. $12

LUIGI RUSTICHELLI, Ed. *Seminario sul racconto*. Vol 16. Narrative. $10

LEWIS TURCO. *Shaking the Family Tree*. Vol 15. Memoirs. $9

LUIGI RUSTICHELLI, Ed. *Seminario sulla drammaturgia*. Vol 14. Theater/Essays. $10

FRED GARDAPHÈ. *Moustache Pete is Dead! Long Live Moustache Pete!*. Vol 13. Oral Literature. $10

JONE GAILLARD CORSI. *Il libretto d'autore. 1860 – 1930*. Vol 12. Criticism. $17

HELEN BAROLINI. *Chiaroscuro: Essays of Identity*. Vol 11. Essays. $15

PICARAZZI & FEINSTEIN, Eds. *An African Harlequin in Milan*. Vol 10. Theater/Essays. $15

JOSEPH RICAPITO. *Florentine Streets & Other Poems*. Vol 9. Poetry. $9

FRED MISURELLA. *Short Time*. Vol 8. Novella. $7

NED CONDINI. *Quartettsatz*. Vol 7. Poetry. $7

ANTHONY JULIAN TAMBURRI, Ed. *Fuori: Essays by Italian/American Lesbiansand Gays*. Vol 6. Essays. $10

ANTONIO GRAMSCI. P. Verdicchio. Trans. & Intro. *The Southern Question*. Vol 5.Social Criticism. $5

DANIELA GIOSEFFI. *Word Wounds & Water Flowers*. Vol 4. Poetry. $8

WILEY FEINSTEIN. *Humility's Deceit: Calvino Reading Ariosto Reading Calvino*. Vol 3. Criticism. $10

PAOLO A. GIORDANO, Ed. *Joseph Tusiani: Poet. Translator. Humanist*. Vol 2. Criticism. $25

ROBERT VISCUSI. *Oration Upon the Most Recent Death of Christopher Columbus*. Vol 1. Poetry.